THE

BURDEN

OF

GRAVITY

Caitlin Press Inc.
8100 Alderwood Road,
Halfmoon Bay, BC V0N 1Y1
www.caitlin-press.com

Text design by Sarah Corsie
Cover design by Monica Miller
Cover image D-04135 courtesy of the Royal BC Museum and Archives
Printed in Canada

Caitlin Press Inc. acknowledges financial support from the Government of Canada and the Canada Council for the Arts, and the Province of British Columbia through the British Columbia Arts Council and the Book Publisher's Tax Credit.

Library and Archives Canada Cataloguing in Publication
The burden of gravity : poems / by Shannon McConnell.
McConnell, Shannon, 1983- author.
Includes bibliographical references.
Canadiana 2020022395X | ISBN 9781773860282 (softcover)
LCSH: Woodlands School (New Westminster, B.C.)—Poetry. | LCSH: Children with disabilities—Institutional care—British Columbia—New Westminster—Poetry. | LCSH: Inmates of institutions—British Columbia—New Westminster—Poetry.
LCC PS8625.C66 B87 2020 | DDC C811/.6—dc23

THE BURDEN OF GRAVITY

poems

Shannon McConnell

CAITLIN PRESS

In memory,
Ian McConnell (1943–1985)
Mary Kantor (1920–2001)

Contents

Introduction

This collection explores the lives of fictionalized residents and the complex legacy of Woodlands School, a former institution in New Westminster, British Columbia. Woodlands School opened in 1878 as the Provincial Lunatic Asylum and later transitioned to a custodial training school for children with various disabilities in 1950. Shortly after Woodlands' closure in 1996, public accusations from former residents and their families began to make headlines claiming they had suffered physical, verbal, sexual, mental and emotional abuse. In the early 2000s volunteers recovered cemetery gravestones from various locations in the Lower Mainland including a retaining wall, ravine, and off-site construction projects. In 2007, Woodlands Memorial Garden was built on the former cemetery property displaying the recovered gravestones on memorial walls. The last remaining section of Woodlands, the Centre Block Tower, was demolished in 2011.

Confined Sp/Faces

Stones

1958

The last body covered,
patted with shovels, the final
gravestone, placed.
All those who came after,
unclaimed, transported to the university.
Cadavers.

1977

The hospital board claimed
the sick and elderly didn't
want to see—
rows of death markers
from their windows, their future.

Eighteen hundred gravestones
relocated into the city.

Staff used some stones to build
a retaining wall behind the school.
Autumn rains seeped into
the soil, dislodging
the slabs, tumbling them
into the creek, submerged.

1986

Playing in her front yard, a young girl pulled
loose one of the stones from the pathway.
She wiped the dirt off,
perplexed by the letters and numbers.
Her father dug out a hundred
more from their driveway.

Visitors discover the patio
behind the school, where staff gathered
for barbecues, was a puzzle
of levelled stones, forced pieces,
some face up.

1999

Five hundred stones recovered.
Every chunk and fragment rescued
regardless of size, shape or integrity.

While preparing to convert
the cemetery to a memorial garden
nine stones are discovered,
forgotten in the purge,
left concealed in the solitude
of fallen tree branches, overgrown
grass and moss.

2007

Survivors gather at the garden,
sombre, despite the steady squeal
of power tools, condos rising across the street.

They congregate, hands gripping
tissues, walking through the park.
They pause, read each name
on the rows and rows and rows
of inset stones and plaques.

Wedged between the rows,
an eight-foot block of granite.
Its eerie black surface, buffed
of imperfections, holds their gaze, aged
reflections. Below it, sunken
into the dirt, one new stone, inscribed:
respect.

Amazing Grace

Sunday morning breaks
the minister's wife
from her bedside prayers.
She pulls her hair into
a slick bun, zips into
her floral dress that falls
above her ankles. She holds
her black folder between her gold cross
and folded arms as she navigates
through patients gathering
at the medication window.

She sits on the rickety piano bench
and fans out tattered hymns,
extends her fingers over the chipped keys.
Her body ticks through
chord changes. Her hands retrace
melodies and refrains fused
in her joints like wooden pews.
She waits for the congregation's amen
as the last chord of the cadence
reverberates off the walls.

Cathode Rays

Alone in the ward two boys lie
in their beds, limbs constricted against
their bodies like twisted tree branches.

They let their eyes relax, watch
the scattered black and white
patterns and shapes form
and fade into hockey rinks
and muscle cars and backyard fires
and playground swings and shooting stars
and ice cream sundaes and sidewalk chalk drawings
and loosened knots in twisted branches.

Across the room
white noise hisses
from the small
television set.

Circles

He walks laps for hours.
His tattered sneakers have
worn a circle into the grass.

Children gather to watch
his hunched shoulders,
strained neck and arms'
rhythmic sway.

Soft words jumble on his tongue
as children try to block his path.
He passes them on the inside,
returning to his track
unfazed.

The children whisper
about the boy
whose parents chained
him to a tree, still unable
to stop the spinning.

Name: Paul█████████
Age: Fifteen
Gender: Male
Diagnosis: ██████████████████
Medication: ████████████████

Ward Occurrences:

The swaying branches
temporary eclipse the sun
a cool brushing over pale skin
not felt through pane.

The Burden of Gravity

From behind the pane
of his ward, Paul watches
a colony of seagulls glide
up from the Fraser. Their mocking
scatters. Paul longs
to detach from the burden
of gravity, hollow his bones,
sprout dark feathers all over
his smooth adolescent skin.
He's eager to join
the other birds on the green
sun-bleached shingles outside
his window; silent
and crouching between
folded wings, waiting
for freedom's lifting breath.

Lunch Time

All the seats at the round dining room table
are filled with young girls, all with the same
haircut—an uneven bob with severe bangs.
Their eyes and hands impatiently wander
along the straight edges of the red
and white-checkered plastic tablecloth.
A boy their age mutely walks around
the tables handing out bowls of food, two
at a time. The new girl stares at the beige
chunks in the bowl, waiting for a spoon.
The other girls, thin after years of such soup,
hastily scoop chunk after chunk into their mouths
with their hands, glancing over
their shoulders before licking their fingers.

Little Pink Pills

At one in the afternoon
the children of Ward 42
are asleep on foam mats
scattered across the floor.
Arms and legs sprawled
like birds dropped
from the sky.
Two nurses circulate around
the maze of children, pausing
to watch their chests slowly rise
and fall. A couple of children snore
loudly, letting out drones that swirl around
the room. A nurse puts her hand
in front of their mouths, feeling
the hot breath on her skin.
Makes a note.
Dr. S will be pleased.

Window Still

Paul stands on the windowsill
behind a pulled drape. The afternoon
sun warms his bare feet. His arms
are stretched skyward, palms pressed
against the corner window frame. Seafoam
drapes brush against his hair, fallen
across his forehead.

Over his shoulder he can see
children in the courtyard, kicking
a partially deflated ball. One
young boy spots him, finger pointed, mouth
calling attention to the window boy. Paul
holds a finger up to his lips, quiet. The boy
lowers his hand, still watching,
grinning.

Paul hears the squeak
of rubber soles, the nurse,
opening the cupboards, the closet,
lifting the mattress on the bed,
checking all his usual places.

His calves and biceps burn.

Disbursement of Medication

A dulled rainbow of pills
divided into paper cups, matching
each cup to a patient card.

She enters the dining hall
holding the tray of pills, the children's
chatter settles and their eyes watch
as she meets an outstretched leg
in her path, and as her knee
buckles, she catches his smirk.
Pills waterfall from her tray.

Rubber Room

"Gentle with knocks,"
the head nurse reminds,
"It's part of the job."

She balances the tray, shifts
her weight to her toes, a quick
glance through the slit of window.

She doesn't want to disturb
the body curled in the middle of straw
filled mattress, fists clenching gown.

Perspiration dampens
her spine, sticks to starched whites
as she pushes
the door, dishes rattle. She holds
her breath, steadies herself:
three steps in.

The bed creaks as the rocking
body releases a crescendo of moans.

She drops the tray on the floor
turns her back, and sprints:
three steps out.

She leans against the door, firmly
pulled shut behind her. Feels
the door reverberate as the tray
smashes against it. Steadies herself
adjusts her starched whites, calms her pace.

Name: Winifred ███████ (Winnie)
Age: Eight
Gender: Female
Diagnosis: ███████████
Medication: ██████████

Ward Occurrences:

She holds her legs
against her chest. Gazes
at the cloud-marked sky.
A plane threads through patches
of cotton, melts
into the sun.

Wallflower

Winnie sits facing
the wall, light blue

peeling paint, two pigtails dangling
down her back. The other girls

brush each other's hair
with their fingers, while

stifling coughs, they sneer, hurl
insults at Winnie's head. She wipes

her dark bangs from her eyes, her mouth
on her cotton dress sleeve. Each slowly

rounded sentence on her lips recounts
her every action of the morning.

She rubs her chest, suppressing
coughs and swift rising secrets, saved

for the blue, peeling wall
her oldest friend.

Boys Bathroom: Morning

The boys of Ward 71
line up outside the bathroom
exchanging nervous looks
between the male nurse's
angry shouts. The boys press
their shoulders against
the bare white wall. Some wipe
absent sleep from their eyes,
while others plug their ears
with their fingers.

The nurse appears in the doorway
holding Jack up by his shirt collar,
pants heavy, soaked around his ankles.
The nurse pushes him into the hall,
hisses, "That's what happens to boys
who take their time pissing." Jack
collapses onto the floor, legs scalded,
blisters bubbling up
his thighs. The boys watch,
his eyes, cracked red
and swollen, as muffled cries
escape the corners
of his mouth.

Secrets

A teacher's aide carries a sheep
across the courtyard to a circle of ten
small children, his thick beard blending
into its wool. As he kneels down
in the centre of the circle, the children's wild hands
grab at the legs and body of the indifferent ewe.

The children dig their fingers into
the greyed overgrown clumps of wool,
squeezing the coarse coat. They take turns
whispering into pale ears
that flutter from the touch of their smooth cheeks
and warm breath. From time to time,
the sheep turns its head
towards the secret.

Keys

belt loop
leather strap
metal ring
falls heavy
against
his white pant
leg, thigh,
each step
one door
closer

Name: Michael ███████████

Age: Sixteen

Gender: Male

Diagnosis: ------------

Medication: -------------

Ward Occurrences:

In the middle of the ward Michael sits

in a wheelchair, one leg crossed
over the other, hands pulled into
the sleeves of his red sweatshirt.
His sandy complexion
faded as past summers.

He stares at the round-headed children singing
in a circle, clapping out of time. A confused
joy floats in their eyes. Michael
mouths the words along
with the children, remembers being
small and gazing skyward
as he scrambled higher, letting the coarse bark
stain his hands. Michael wishes
he could gather the children, teach them
to climb, branch by branch, leaves
brushing through their hair and down
their cheeks, seeing how small
everything looks
below.

The Playroom

The small kids claw
at each other's shirt collars
grasp for wrists and matted hair
trying to claim the small wooden tunnel—
the only place to hide.

The bigger kids climb
the large wooden platform, reach
the window, press palms
and foreheads against the glass
each breath a circle
clouding the view.

Sin Bin

The boys and girls in the class stare
hard at the papers on their desks,
avoiding eye contact with Winnie
as the teacher drags her
by the collar of her dress. Winnie cries,
the bruises across her ribs
haven't healed from last time.

The teacher lifts Winnie up, her nails digging
into the skin under Winnie's armpits. She lowers
Winnie into the table with the hole in the middle,
lets her legs drop
until the sharp wooden edges press tight
against her inflamed ribs.

Winnie faces the class, arms stretched,
grasping for the outer edges
of the table, unable to pull
herself out. She slaps the top
of the table, pleads at the ears
and eyes of the kids all around,
but they refuse to look up.

Above her, a drawing, white ink
on black paper, a baby in a diaper
stares down, a thick halo
above its head.

Prohibited

Mother, May I? Capture the Flag. Simon Says, Kick the Can. Ghosts in the

Graveyard—Heads Up, Seven Up. Cat's Cradle, Red Rover, Marco Polo. Telephone,

Red Light, Green Light, Hopscotch, Marbles. Hide and Hide and Hide and Hide and—

Clipped Wings

Paul sneaks to the roof,
leans against the cement
centre block. His wavy hazelnut
hair deciphers the wind's
direction. He steadies himself,
his left arm outstretched
while taking uneasy steps along
the slanted shingles. His right
arm is pulled close
to his chest in a blinding white
cast, a consequence
of his last rooftop appearance.

One by one, children
on the playground slow
their game of tag,
crane their necks
upwards. Some point
fingers, others snicker
at the boy staggering
along the roof. None
of the children run
to call a nurse, every pair
of eyes eager
to see if the broken boy
will fall again.

Name: Elizabeth ██████████ (Miss Taylor)
Age: █
Gender: Female
Diagnosis: ██████████ ██████
Medication: ██████ ██████ ████ ███████

Ward Occurrences:

Scarves and gloves
in summer, like they do
in Hollywood. A woman
never tells her age, keeps
her lips and gloves pulled tight.

Miss Taylor

The hot lights of Hollywood don't
shine in these halls. Elizabeth insists

the nurses call her Miss Taylor. She
makes them coffee, always takes hers

black. Red stains pressed
against the lip of her mug. They don't

know where she gets the lipstick. She won't speak
of the trail of men she's left scattered

along the coast nor the films
her face has graced. No, she won't

bore the nurses with Hollywood
gossip. They prefer their balding husbands

and afternoon soaps to illuminated marquees.
She tells the nurses that she's shaken

out the names of past lovers,
lurking in her hair. She's grown

tired of the big screen, no longer wants
scripted words in her mouth. Her own

are stronger proof than in the drinks sipped
with Hudson or Dean. She hears the nurses

behind half-closed doors share
that Miss Taylor has a face only

the blind would pay to see. She brushes the wrinkles
from her dingy black dress, adjusts her fading pearls,

she's never been one to give a damn.

Falling

Paul tells the nurses
he was born falling, arms and legs
outstretched to open air pouring
over his freshly birthed skin, thin
wisps of hair curling at the base of his skull.
He needs to climb, explore,
leap, a biological response to the call
to adventure packed into his cells
at conception. He's not afraid
of heights or the moment
his sneakers and body disconnect
from the earth, suspended
and separate from the others, bonded
with all other winged beings. He
only fears contact, gravity's
reminder.

Smoke Scare

The fire alarm beats in a high register—
residents evacuate to the lawn.
Men in dark suits dig their hands
into their pockets, anchoring themselves
between residents carried
from their beds in white sheets.

The children, left on their backs, gaze
toward the building, bewildered by the brisk
morning air. They settle, rest their eyes
on slouching mountains
descending into foothills they'll never see.

Beauty Secrets

After breakfast Miss Taylor climbs
the floors, one hand clutching
the rail, the other holding
a saucer of leftover milk. Her knees
rub against her faded yellow
nightgown as she lifts each foot
up to the next step, pausing
to steady her fluttering
hand, each drop precious.
She places the saucer in the sun
on the laundry room sill. "Sour milk
won't fix your curdled face," scoffs
another resident, folding clothes. The rest
of the room averts their words, continues
their sorting over the low rumbles
of the machines.

In the evening she retrieves
the saucer, places it on the lip
of her sink, closes her eyes, dips
her bony fingers in the thick,
warm milk, massaging it in circles
over baby crow's feet and unearned
laugh lines. She stares
at the mirror, eyes clouded
with determination as milk
drips from her chin.

Grounded

Five Ward 71 boys trail behind
Mr. Thomas, their hands tucked

into their windbreaker pockets, chilled
as they walk in a line across the courtyard

towards the fence. Mr. Thomas holds open
the school's large metal gate, the boys pass through,

ducking under his stare. The morning breeze raises
goosebumps beneath their close-shaved scalps.

They walk down to the curve of McBride,
gather beneath the rounded wing

and oval engine of a Beechcraft Model 18 airplane.
Mr. Thomas slaps down a boy's hand

reaching to feel the large metal sheets and rivets.
They walk around the plane,

the smallest boy counts aloud, the four small windows
across the fuselage, stopping to read

two black bubble lettered words
printed on its body, "*Woodlands Airline.*"

The boys stare at the jutting wings,
dream about the sunny side of the clouds,

jagged edges of continents, not two cement blocks
at their feet that ground the plane

air leaking through
the cracked rubber.

Buntzen Lake Field Trip

Paul crouches at the end
of the dock, balances
on his heels as he watches
his classmates scatter

along the shore. Their teachers
relax at a picnic table, cigarettes lit,
smoke and gossip circling. Paul
rolls up his sleeves, three flat folds
up each arm. Quietly lies on the dock
letting the wood planks press
against his ribs. Dips his hands
into the water, fingers swaying
in the shallow waves like worms
dangling below the surface. Roaming
mosquitos buzz past his ears, fish dart
around his fingers. He holds his breath

and hands still. A trout circles
and Paul grabs for the fish, its body
thrashing as he grips behind its gills,
feeling the cartilage and bone under
his fingertips. He yanks
the fish from the water, as pain flashes
across his back, a teacher's heavy sole
presses against his spine, pushing the air
from his lungs.

Work

Important work to be done.

Michael gathers the duller children
in the dayroom, dumps a bucket
full of nuts, bolts, screws, nails
onto the table that scatter like jacks.
The children grin at the pile
fidget their hands.

Michael lines up four mason jars.
Important work to be done.

The children grab at the pieces,
curled threads and rounded edges
under their fingertips.

Nuts with nails with bolts with screws with
nails with bolts with screws with nuts.

When the table is clear
Michael dumps the contents
of the jars back into the bucket.
Shakes it, the scraping of metal
on metal, until he dumps the mess
back onto the table.

Important work to be done.

Name: Sharon ███████

Age: Seventeen

Gender: Female

Diagnosis: ███ █████████ ██████ ████████

Medication: ████ ████████ ██████

Ward Occurrences:

Tucked into a sheet, resting
on her side, her eyes trace
along the bottom of a nurse's uniform.
Line space line space line space
line space line space line space line.

We've Got a Violent One Here

Sharon stares at the five slits
in the heating vent.

She has watched the days darken

multiple times since the nurse tied her
into a straightjacket and threw her
against the wall

of the stark,
                   empty room.

She lies on her side,
                   elbow pressed

against her ribs. Her face
is chafed from the carpet

burns when she tries to pull
herself out of the puddle of piss.

She listens to the hum of warm air pouring out

the vent and grows jealous
of the daylight as it creeps across the floor,
in long ropes, hangs itself
from the bars of the window.

Paging Nurse Dawn

Did you know it was him when you found Debbie hunched over the toilet, her adolescent arms trembling as she held the curve of the porcelain?

Did you know it was him when you rubbed slow circles between her shoulder blades?

Did you know it was him when you steadied her, pulled dirty cotton nightgown over her head, gazed down at the growing convex in her taut skin?

Did you know it was him

again.

Detention

Michael and Paul sit across from each other,
locked in a 8 x 10 room, for fighting.

From the window, barred,
they hear other children on the playground:

the creak of chains,
shoes across gravel,
careful laughter.

The boys ball up their socks, toss them
back and forth back and forth back and forth.

They watch the sun stretch the bar's shadow
across the yellowing linoleum
until night pulls the black bars back into the window.

Biters

He remembers the pliers, hovering
above his face. He fought
against the arm and leg restraints chafing
his skin. Now he leans against the cracked
porcelain and stares into the mirror.

He cannot recognize his own face, except for
his blue eyes, now encircled
by burgundy bruises, like staring through
binoculars. The rest of his face, a blend
of purple patches crawling up
his swollen cheeks, where the white-
masked doctor grabbed his jaw—
"this is how we fix the biters."

He tries to open his mouth,
but his lips are bruised, only a thin
slit separating them. He winces,
cautious, runs the tip
of his tongue over his empty gums.

Shadows in the Night

From her bed at the end
of the ward, Sharon lies
listening to another resident
pacing between the rows of beds.

Sharon watches the woman's shadow
cross over the end of her bed,
trailing murmurs.

Rarely do any of the women
on the ward sleep at night,
their wails and midnight bickering,
interspersed with muffled pillow screams.

Sharon watches the pacing
woman, praying that she
finds her own bed
instead of Sharon's again.

Name: Edward ████████ (Eddie)
Age: Ten
Gender: Male
Diagnosis: ████ ███ ██ ████ █████
Medication: ██ █ ███ ██ ████ ██████

Ward Occurrences:

He sits for hours
in a hard chair, rolling
his die-cast Thunderbird over
his defective legs. The aqua blue
body rolling over shallow hills
stuck in the valley, motor crooning.

Steps

In an empty hall the nurses hold
Eddie like a marionette.
One nurse holds a wrist, the other
a fistful of Eddie's sagging pants.
The women move in slow motion
hoping each muscle will absorb
the swing of his leg, the bend
of his arm, and memorize each movement
filing them into the folds of his brain.

At the end of the hall, Eddie's muscles
go limp and the nurses lift his weary head
up off his chest, his eyes dulled
with defeat. They turn around,
point him down the hall for the slow
hobble back to the ward.

Patrol

Michael, the tallest boy
stands against the door frame,
one hand grasping
the rounded knob. Hair combed,
teeth brushed, shoes
polished.
He watches through
the safety glass
window.

Fred, the toughest boy, sits
in a metal folding chair, legs stretched
out and resting on the corner
of a bed. He watches the boys scramble
to dress while taking long drags
off his cigarette.

Michael carefully watches
through the glass, his tongue
acidic, dry. The red circles
on his left arm remind him
he only has seconds
to warn Fred the uniforms
are coming.

Terranaut

Paul takes one small step
towards the television,
pressing his hand against
the static-filled screen.
He touches the moon
as Armstrong, 400,000 kms away
stands in dust.

Paul longs to be the loneliest man
in the universe, free
from the lunacy of gravity,
among the basaltic plains.

Fill his pockets
with moon rocks, take one giant leap
towards the marble swirl
of weightless and disoriented
cosmic debris.

Hallway

Nurse Maureen stands
holding Eddie against
her white uniform, his sobs
saturate. His white helmet
presses against her chest as he leans
into her. She rubs his back, cradles
his pained joints in her arms,
holds up his ten-year-old body
as other patients walk past, staring.
She wipes his damp cheeks
with her thumb, and waits
for his vacant eyes to fill again.

Jars

Sharon helps in the children's ward
changing diapers, feeding open mouths
and calming wailing babies. She waits
for the nurses to step out of the ward
then takes every jar of Vaseline left
on counters or shelves and throws them
in the garbage. Each missing jar
a way of making sure the nurses
don't use it on the little kids
like her father did on her.

Sidelines

A nurse asks Eddie to join
the circle of boys in the middle
of the classroom.
Eddie stays curled
up in his chair, pushed against the wall.
His feet pulled tight up onto the chair,
arms drawn close
trying to fold into himself.

Eddie pulls at his collar and eyes
the diagonal rip across
the vinyl cushion of the
chair beside him. The foam
poking out, a neglected wound.

Name: Margaret ███████████ (Maggie)
Age: Fifty-Three
Gender: Female
Diagnosis: ████████████████
Medication: ██████

Ward Occurrences:

From her wheelchair she watches
the white jackets pace
between patients, cigarettes burn
between their fingers. She inhales
the scent like smooth acid, drawing
in a temporary calm, a slow roll
of hand tremors.

Tethered

Maggie in her wheelchair, babbling
through her fingertips held in
her mouth. Her free hand pulls
at the thin blanket covering her,
two corners tied behind her neck.
Her gown sticks to her backside
with salve meant to sooth her
oozing sores, instead smears
all over her wheelchair, tethered
with a soft restraint to the wooden railing
behind. She slouches, touching bare toes
to the urine puddle below, rolling forward
and back, until the wheels bump
against the wall. Her short dark hair
is clipped neatly, and brushes against her
forehead when she tilts her head to watch
other patients avert their eyes and walk close
to the other wall, their fingertips brushing
against the rail.

When Did You Know You Could Let Go?

Your hands and bandages
over Winnie's hands

Cover the deep scratches,
compress her urge to pry,
keep the blood flowing.

How long did you hum soft shushes?

Your calming timbre
for her ears only, slows the drip
of blood onto your white uniform.

How long were you going to stand in the hall, Nurse Dawn?

Custodian

Stacks of tattered boxes.
He heaves another
towards the edge. Pauses,
rubs his throbbing lower back,
returns to the cramped storage room
for more. Some mornings
there are many, others none.
Box by box, he rips open
folded flaps, tearing down
the corners. He sifts through letters,
clothing, crisp magazines, tossing them
below into the steep-sided narrow
gorge. Opens envelopes,
cards and wallets, stuffs
folded five-dollar bills
into his worn back pockets.
The front he fills with rings,
watches and necklaces. He shakes
the empty box, listens
for shifting coins, trapped
between the bottom flaps.
When the last box is done,
dissected and discarded, he lights
a match. Tosses the stretching flame
below, the whole bank ignites.

Waste Not

One plot can fit
many children
if you bury
them standing up.

Stash

For weeks Sharon has been sneaking
bread and muffins from the cafeteria
and trading them for an older girl's diet pills.

Under her sheets, Sharon counts
the pills, hopes that soon
she'll have enough to escape.

Name: Deborah ██████████ (Debbie)
Age: Twenty-Seven
Gender: Female
Diagnosis: ██████
Medication: --------------

Ward Occurrences:

Lying on her stomach on the grass,
holding her hand over the tips
of the blades, each green strand
traces the creases of her palm.

She picks the blades one by one,
building a pile in her hand to hide
in her pocket for later.

Debbie listens for the night

Nurse's shoes, weighted taps
passing the door. Debbie
slips her worn wool cardigan
over her bony shoulders, slowly
reaching for the cool metal
frame at the end of her bed.
Her fingertips seek
what she can no longer see:
> bevelled dresser corners
> metal bedframe
> square table
> metal bedframe
> porcelain sink
> metal bedframe
> doorknob.

Turn.

Debbie's stomach burns, empty
as she listens for shaking
keys, and distant voices.
Her fingertips trace over:
> peeling paint
> bulletin board
> railing
> gurney
> water fountain
> wheelchair
> doorframe.

Turn.

Debbie inhales the scent
of thick lemon cleaner along
the countertops. She traces
her fingertips over flat
drawer handles, carefully
stepping along the tiled floor.
She opens a cupboard, leans in
to smell for the creamy
package of butter. She reaches
for the second shelf, digging
her fingers into the soft
brick. She pulls it down, sits
on the floor, her feet pressing
down on the corners
of the square tiles. She scoops
smooth clumps into her mouth, a layer
of elation spreading around her lips
as she licks her fingers
and waits.

Bath

Did you run the water first?
Test it on your wrist?

Did you lather soap on a washcloth?
Let her gently wash her own limbs without flinching?

Did you keep your eyes on hers?
Detract from the shame of bruises down her thighs?

Did you wrap a clean towel around her skinny shoulders?
Wipe the damp hair off her forehead?

Did you turn your back?
Let her remove her own body?

On Days Without Rain

The nurses divide the residents
into groups, taking them
to the courtyard to walk
hand in hand, grown ups
and children.

Sharon is stuck
with an old man's
sausage fingers
and clammy palms.
He squeezes her hand,
her knuckles rolling
under her skin.

A teenage girl,
two years her junior,
pulls on Sharon's other arm,
grasping her left hand
tight, digging
her freshly chewed nails
into the creases
of Sharon's palm.

They cross the courtyard
like a chain of clumsy paper dolls.
Sharon scans the grounds for trees
with thick branches hanging over
the fence, waiting for the nurse
to turn them back.

Rounds: Thursday – 23:47

During the nightshift Nurse Maureen walks
the dim halls, flashlight beam swaying
as she hums. She pulls out keys,
unlocks the door to the ward—
blind and deaf boys.
The syncopated sounds of sleep
surround her as she shines the light
on each bed, outlining
their shoulders. Their chests rise and fall,
rise and fall, as she counts her way
through the ward. She smells
the stench of rum. Her eyes catch
on the last bed, streaming eyes.
The light shines
along the bed. White pants,
black belt, white shirt—untucked,
and a startled bearded face.

Rounds: Friday – 06:13

Nurse Maureen waits in her supervisor's office.
Stares at the mismatched frames
of diplomas, desk stacked
with papers and files,
coffee rings.

She wants to close her eyes, fall asleep,
and give in to the morning sun
on her face. But every time
she closes her eyes she sees
the helpless boy, eyes wet with fear.

The door opens, she turns to see
Dr. S and HIM enter, his averted eyes.
The stench of rum engulfs
the room. Maureen
covers her mouth, holding back
the contents of her stomach.

Dr. S leans against the front of his desk,
arms crossed—irritated. His face is
worn, sleepless. She glances over
at HIM, fresh white shirt, no creases.
His hands clench the arms of his chair
beside her.

"What do you think you saw?" Dr. S snaps.

Before she can respond, she sees HIM
in her periphery, syringe in hand.
A sharp sensation spreads
through her leg.

Rounds: Friday – 07:03

Nurse Maureen comes to, her vision
                                blurred.
She reaches
            for her glasses,
but her arms are tied
                        down and she's rolling
through
a hall,
doors and rails
and white shirts,
everything in doubles.

She tries to sit up,
                    feels a firm hand
push her shoulders
down, as warmth spreads
through the IV tubes
                    taped to her arm.

Her eyelids flutter.
                    She stares
at fluorescent lights

reminds her of driving
through the Massey tunnel,
burrowing

            under the weight
            of the river,
            the Fraser River.

Rounds: Sanatorium – Friday – 23:56

Maureen awakes to the wall breathing.
At the foot of her bed, Dali's Jesus hangs
on a hypercube, arms extended,
fists clenched, head slumped
to the right. He's dying to know what's left.
.She feels violins in her lungs, connecting
legato melodies as she exhales.
She tries to hold her breath,
but the notes gather
on the back of her tongue and when she parts
her lips, each refrain escapes in trills.
Bursts of light strobe around her and she reaches
for something concrete. She's lost in the steam
rising from her forearms, fogging her face.
When did her eyelids became transparent?

"Hello?"

"Valerie?"

"Mom?"

"They've locked me up."

"They say I'm

crazy."

"You've got to come

and get me."

"Do you hear

me?"

"The
San."

"Valerie?"

"Hello?"

Escape

Dirt between her teeth,
gritty and metallic. The taste
of a midnight break for the gates.
Afternoon rain shower, standing water,
Sharon's soles slapping against soft soil,
        a misstep   a slip
her face smashing and sinking
into the sod, waiting for
the tight grip of an orderly
around her ankles, dragging
her through the dewy lawn,
the emerald blades raking
her cheeks.

Geranium Red

They take the hospital gown off,
ease Miss Taylor's head back down
onto the cool marble slab,
lift her, pull the clean floral
dress over her head. Each nurse takes
a turn sliding an arm through
a sleeve, tugs the dress down
her cold back. They lift
her hips and tug
at the fabric until the hem
of the dress rests above
her ankles.

One nurse brushes
Miss Taylor's hair,
tucks the thin white
hair behind her cold ears. The other
nurse wrings out a cold cloth,
wipes the thick layer
of the red lipstick
off Miss Taylor's lips.

They fold her arms across
her chest, close her eyelids,
check their watches.
There's still time for a quick cigarette.

Erased Pl/Faces

Did You Think No One Would Notice?

Did you think their bodies would never speak
of the damage held between ribs and lungs?

Did you think you could conceal their scars
with long sleeves and pant legs rolled down?

Did you think you could hold their silence
like kittens under water?

Barbecue Patio

That summer you built the staff a barbecue patio out of residents' gravestones.

Did you bask in the cool breeze flowing up from the Fraser?

Did you flip ground beef burgers on the grill?

Did you snuff out your cigarettes on their name or the year they died?

Columbia Street

Penitentiary	Woodlands
smokestack	smokestack
Woodlands	Penitentiary
watchtower	watchtower
Penitentiary	Woodlands
dirt track	dirt track
Woodlands	Penitentiary
dark peaked roof	dark peaked roofs
Penitentiary	Woodlands
parking lot	parking lot
Woodlands	Penitentiary
high stone walls	high stone walls
Penitentiary	Woodlands
flat top roofs	flat top roofs
Woodlands	Penitentiary
interlocked buildings	interlocked buildings
Penitentiary	Woodlands
metal gates	metal gates
Woodlands	Penitentiary

Demolition Pantoum

"I was sixteen for twenty years. By September I will be a ghost."
                                        Lucie Brock-Broido, *"A Girl Ago."*

I was sixteen. For twenty years
remains
shivered down my spine.
There will be no closure.

Remains
a single building: the Centre Block Tower.
There will be no closure
in the dust.

A single building, the Centre Block Tower.
The crumbling white
in the dust—
a symbol without substance.

The crumbling white
destruction brought relief,
a symbol. Without substance,
I was sixteen for twenty years.

Nomenclature: 1878 – Present

Provincial Lunatic Asylum Provincial Lunatic Asylum Provincial Lunatic Asylum
Provincial Lunatic Asylum Provincial Lunatic Asylum Provincial Lunatic Asylum
Provincial Lunatic Asylum Provincial Lunatic Asylum Provincial Lunatic Asylum
Provincial Asylum for the Insane Provincial Asylum for the Insane
Provincial Asylum for the Insane Provincial Asylum for the Insane
Provincial Asylum for the Insane Provincial Asylum for the Insane
Provincial Hospital for the Insane Provincial Hospital for the Insane
Provincial Hospital for the Insane Provincial Hospital for the Insane
Provincial Hospital for the Insane Provincial Hospital for the Insane
Woodlands School Woodlands School Woodlands School Woodlands School
Woodlands School Woodlands School Woodlands School Woodlands School
Woodlands School Woodlands School Woodlands School Woodlands School
Woodlands Woodlands Woodlands Woodlands Woodlands Woodlands Woodlands
Woodlands Woodlands Woodlands Woodlands Woodlands Woodlands Woodlands
Centre Block Centre Block Centre Block Centre Block Centre Block Centre Block
Centre Block Centre Block Centre Block Centre Block Centre Block Centre Block
Tower Tower Tower Tower Tower Tower Tower Tower Tower Tower Tower
Tower Tower Tower Tower Tower Tower Tower Tower Tower Tower Tower
Demolition Demolition Demolition Demolition Demolition Demolition Demolition
Demolition Demolition Demolition Demolition Demolition Demolition Demolition

Victoria Hill // Gated Community Victoria Hill // Gated Community Victoria Hill
Victoria Hill // Gated Community Victoria Hill // Gated Community Victoria Hill

The Need To Know

Ombudsman,

How many nights did you stare
                        stare
                    stare
at files,
            ceiling tiles,
                        trauma circles

growing around your eyes?

Headstones

decades, concrete

wooden block letters — buried or ripped out

few signs remain.

former residents

the cemetery citizens lie silently grassy

knolls.

the garden

living survivors

those who didn't wait their turn.

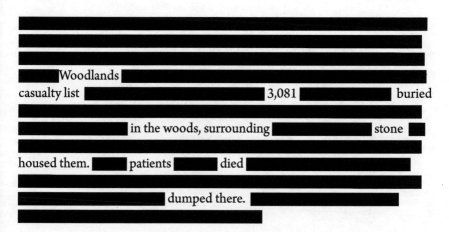

Woodlands
casualty list 3,081 buried
in the woods, surrounding stone
housed them. patients died
dumped there.

Friends Who Didn't

███ thick grove of maples, ████ tardy summer sun, ████ survived

████████████ wept, ██████ the friends who didn't.

The Wrong Side of 1974
(Who Should be Compensated?)

July 31, 1974	August 1, 1974
Hitting	Hitting
Kicking	Kicking
Smacking	Smacking
Slapping	Slapping
Grabbing	Grabbing
Dragging	Dragging
Restraining	Restraining
Pushing	Pushing
Kicking	Kicking
Shoving	Shoving
Violating	Violating

Ø   Prove it.

Compensation Violation Marks

I

kissing or fondling over clothes

mark mark mark mark mark
mark mark mark mark mark

fondling under clothes

mark mark mark mark mark
mark mark mark mark mark
mark mark mark mark mark
mark mark mark mark mark

going without three squares a day

mark mark mark mark mark
mark mark mark mark mark
mark mark mark mark mark
mark mark mark mark mark
mark mark mark mark mark

anal or vaginal intercourse

mark mark mark mark mark
mark mark mark mark mark
mark mark mark mark mark
mark mark mark mark mark
mark mark mark mark mark
mark mark mark mark mark
mark mark mark mark mark
mark mark mark mark mark
mark mark mark mark mark
mark mark mark mark mark
mark mark mark mark mark
mark mark mark mark mark

II

1 -10 marks	up to $9,000
11 - 121 marks	$221,000 and $247,500

III

insulting ▪ demeaning ▬▬▬▬▬▬▬▬▬
▬▬▬▬▬▬▬▬▬▬▬▬
▬ remember ▬▬ pulled ▪ dragged by the hair ▬▬ locked
▬▬ isolation ▬▬▬▬▬▬▬▬
▬▬▬▬▬▬▬▬▬▬▬
▬▬▬▬▬ relive ▬▬▬▬▬ torture ▬
▬▬▬▬▬▬▬▬▬▬
countered ▬▬▬▬▬▬ each ▬▬ $15,000 ▬▬
▬▬▬▬▬▬▬▬▬▬
call it a day ▬▬▬▬▬

Construction

█ New Westminster. █ Woodlands █
█ transforming into Victoria Hill, █
█ home to 3,000 █ The █ community will █
█ support █ new residents.

Construction █ to remember
█ former residents.

█ Former patients █ buried █ on █
site, █ unceremoniously █
█ redeveloped █ and █ forgotten.

Now, the █ Gardens █ remember █
█

█ 3,000 █ died █
█ bodies █
█ unclaimed, █ buried █
█
█

█ dismantled █ grave
markers █
█ found █ in █ a █ creek. █
█ hauled away █
█

"The decision █ the site █ the
headstones █ the
memorial.

reason ▮ removed, ▮

residents ▮

headstones ▮

removed, ▮

▮

advocates ▮ former patients ▮ volunteers began ▮

looking ▮

grave markers ▮ now ▮

incorporated in ▮ the ▮ gardens. ▮ not all ▮ have

been found, ▮ still ▮

buried ▮

"Regardless of ▮ integrity ▮ every piece ▮ every

▮ stone is ▮ meaningful ▮ in these

walls," ▮

repatriate ▮

the ▮ School ▮ the ▮ incidents

▮

"The ▮ shared ▮ experience ▮

▮

stories about ▮ place ▮ The ▮

tears ▮ memories ▮

stories."

▮

former residents ▮

split ▮ connected ▮

buried ▮

displayed.

large black window

frame ▮ window sill ▮ so high ▮

███████████████████████ 'A window too high.' ██████████████████████

███

kids ████ couldn't see ██

███████████████████████████

███ they

go ██████████ touch it. ████ reaction █████████████ powerful. ████

█ reflecting ████████████████████████ image ███████████████████

████ a metaphoric an█ experiential ████ view, █████████ to ████████

touch █████████████

██████████████████ 3,200 names █████████████████████████████

███████████████████████████████ Woodlands ████████████████████

██████ Essondale ██

███████████ Riverview█

"Every ████████████████████████████████ name ████████████████

███

█████████████████████████ buried ███████████████████████████

How to Wash Gravestones

Volunteers gather around the pile.
Cradle gravestones like still-warm, stillborns.
Saturate with water.
Use the softest brush.
Only use a stiffer bristle, if needed.
Start at the bottom and work upward.
Rinse often with water.
Gently scrape away the lichens or moss with a wooden scraper.
Use circular motions.
Rinse the clean area.
Repeat on all sides until clean.

Restoration of Gravestones

Volunteers gather around
the pile. Cradle gravestones
like still-warm, stillborns.
Saturate with ~~water~~ *the past.*
Use the softest ~~brush~~ *touch.*
Only use ~~a stiffer bristle~~ *pressure,* if needed.
Start at the bottom ~~and work upward~~ *with hushed words.*
Rinse often with ~~water~~ *bouts of insomnia.*
Gently scrape away the lichens or moss with ~~a wooden scraper~~ *self-blame.*
~~Use~~ *uncover* circular ~~motions~~ *scars.*
~~Rinse~~ *protect* the clean area.
Repeat ~~on all sides~~ *for days* until ~~clean~~ *restored.*

Placeholders

Among the recovered stones,
cracked, eroded and worn.
There are fresh stones,
nameless and smooth.

Unclaimed placeholders
waiting for those who haven't been
retrieved
reclaimed
returned to the cemetery,
cemented.

the dead B.C. hid

here the weeds
grow in

brushed dirt
faded, concrete surface

overlook

erase

Woodlands
long-forgotten
from existence.

neglected
history a graveyard wiped from
memory

stones marked
notorious wooded lands

overgrown

search history Woodlands

didn't exist.

hearses

move

weed-choked,

slope.

time

buried

slight indentations

3,000 graves

obscured

left behind

retain

twist the indignity of

Woodlands

tracking down

names

never found.

recovered used

erasure of lives

names

hidden

the missing

never heard

records, buried

70 years

headstones,

jumbled pile

███████████████████████████████████████

██████████ weep ███████████████████████

███████

██

███████████████

███████████████████████████████████████

███████████████████ 'They will ████████ be forgotten.'

Memorial Drive

Sediment and sturgeons settle below
a tugboat pulling logs, landscape's
leftovers, up the Fraser River.

Along the shoreline the freight-train's dirge
hovers above the percussive
clanking of steel.

Up the hill machinery drones
stacking concrete storey
upon storey extending skyward.

A two-car collision
on the Pattullo clots commuters
along the curve of McBride Blvd

down Memorial Drive
where residents creep through
carbon monoxide, close

their morning eyes to the sharp
reflection of the sun climbing
into their mirror and through

the black-barred window
(too high for other eyes)
drawing shadows on the cement path

as the impatient ones cut through
the garden, eyes on their phones
oblivious to the silence buried
with soil and bones.

Sources

Adolph, Val. *In the Context of Its Time: A History of Woodlands*. Victoria: Govt. of British Columbia, Ministry of Social Services, 1996.

Adolph, Val. *Memories of Woodlands*. Victoria: Govt. of British Columbia, Ministry of Social Services, 1996.

Dauphinais, Carol. *Living with Labels and Lies: A Life Story*. Vancouver: C. Dauphinais, 1997.

de Courcy, Michael. *ASYLUM: a long, last look at Woodlands: 1878 to 2003*. Photography installation, 2003. New Westminster Public Library Art Gallery, New Westminster, BC.

Hume, Mark. "Giving Dignity to the Dead B.C. Tried to Hide from View." *The Globe and Mail*, July 18, 2005.

Inclusion BC. "Woodlands Institution." *Woodlands Institution | Inclusion BC*, Inclusion BC, 2012.

Kane, Laura. "Ex-Residents Cheer as Former B.C. Residential School Is Torn Down." *The Globe and Mail*, October 18, 2011.

McCallum, Dulcie. *The Need to Know: Administrative Review of Woodlands School*. Victoria: Government of British Columbia, Ministry of Children and Family Development, 2001.

McMurchy-Barber, Gina. *Free as a Bird*. Toronto: Dundurn Press, 2010.

McQuillan, Michael. "Woodlands Memorial Taking Shape." *Burnaby NewsLeader*, October 12, 2006.

Scott, Dan. "Photos: Woodlands School History." *Windsor Star*, October 18, 2011, *www.windsorstar.com*.

Thompson, Joey. "Survivors of Woodlands Abuse Still Waiting." *The Province*, June 25, 2007.

"Woodlands Class Action Lawsuit." *Klein Lawyers*, Klein Lawyers.

Notes on the Poems

The line "I was sixteen for twenty years" in the poem "Demolition Pantoum" is borrowed from Lucie Brock-Broido's poem "A Girl Ago."

"Demolition Pantoum" uses lines from "Ex-Residents Cheer as Former B.C. Residential School Is Torn Down." Laura Kane, *The Globe and Mail*. October 18, 2011.

"Headstones", "60 Pages", "Friends Who Didn't", "~~Compensation~~ Violation Marks", "II", and "III" were created from "Survivors of Woodlands abuse still waiting." Joey Thompson, *The Province*. June 25, 2007.

"the dead B.C. hid" was created from "Giving Dignity to the Dead B.C. Tried to Hide from View." Mark Hume, *The Globe and Mail*. July 18, 2005.

"Construction" was created from "Woodlands Memorial Taking Shape." Michael McQuillan, *Burnaby NewsLeader*. October 12, 2006.

These poems were created through researching archival materials; therefore all names are pseudonyms and are not based on specific people.

Acknowledgements

Thank you to my family for their endless love, laughter and support: Violette McConnell, Betty Saucier, Matthew, Marlena, Maddyn and Maclyn McConnell. Also, Ian McConnell, you are forever missed and always remembered.

Special thanks to Jeanette Lynes for her continued guidance, encouragement and support.

Endless thanks and appreciation to my Deeers, who helped me earn my antlers: Danielle Altrogge, Lindsay Kiesman, Katherine Lawrence, Julianna McLean and Cassi Smith. This collection would not have been possible without your feedback and encouragement. You have taught me so much about life and friendship, but most importantly, to never write with my knees together.

Thank you to Shannon McIvor, Lori McClure, Christina Kendall, Kirsten Ickert, Reggie Aulakh, Gina and Chris Geoghegan, Keith Chan, Pete Tozer, and Jaeson Winfield for decades of friendship that continues to grow, near or far.

Thank you to Andrea MacPherson for introducing me to Woodlands, and believing in the potential of the quiet student at the back of the classroom.

Thank you to Elizabeth Philips, for mentoring me during the beginning stages of this manuscript. Your feedback was invaluable and greatly appreciated.

In 2018, "The Burden of Gravity" won second place in the John V. Hicks Long Manuscript Award for Poetry.

"The Burden of Gravity" previously appeared in liberal arts journal, *In Medias Res*.

This manuscript was created while in the Master of Fine Arts in Writing program at the University of Saskatchewan.

About the Author

KEITH CHAN PHOTO

Shannon McConnell is a writer, educator, and musician originally from Vancouver, British Columbia. Her poetry and fiction have appeared in *untethered, The Fieldstone Review, Louden Singletree, In Medias Res, Rat's Ass Review, The Anti-Languorous Project* and more. She holds degrees in English Literature and Education from the University of the Fraser Valley and Simon Fraser University, respectively, and also holds a Master of Fine Arts in Writing and a Master of Arts in History from the University of Saskatchewan. In 2018, she won second place in the John V. Hicks Long Manuscript Award for Poetry.

This book is set in Arno Pro, created by Robert Slimbach.
The text was typeset by Sarah Corsie.

Caitlin Press, 2020.